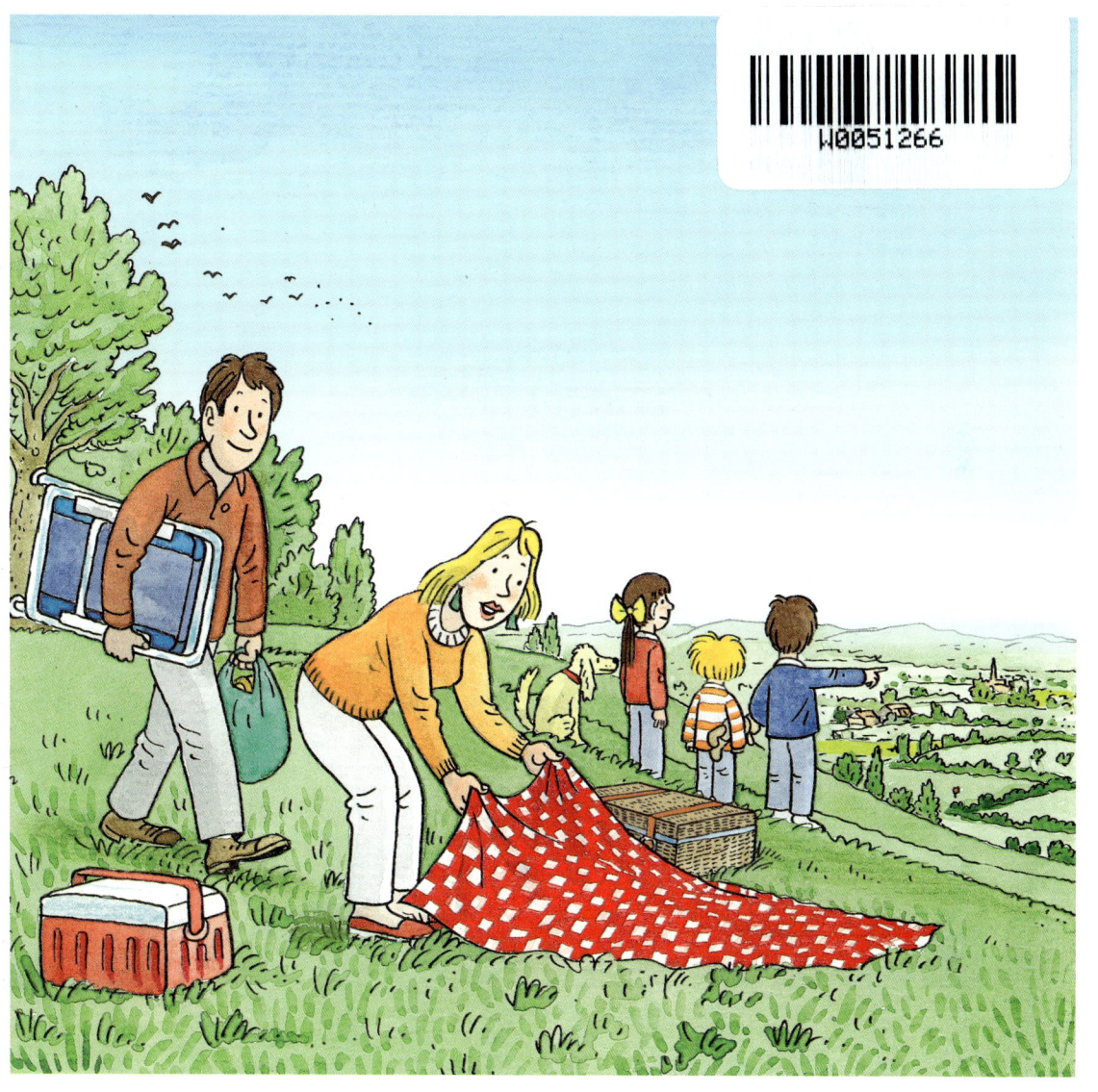

The picnic was up a hill.

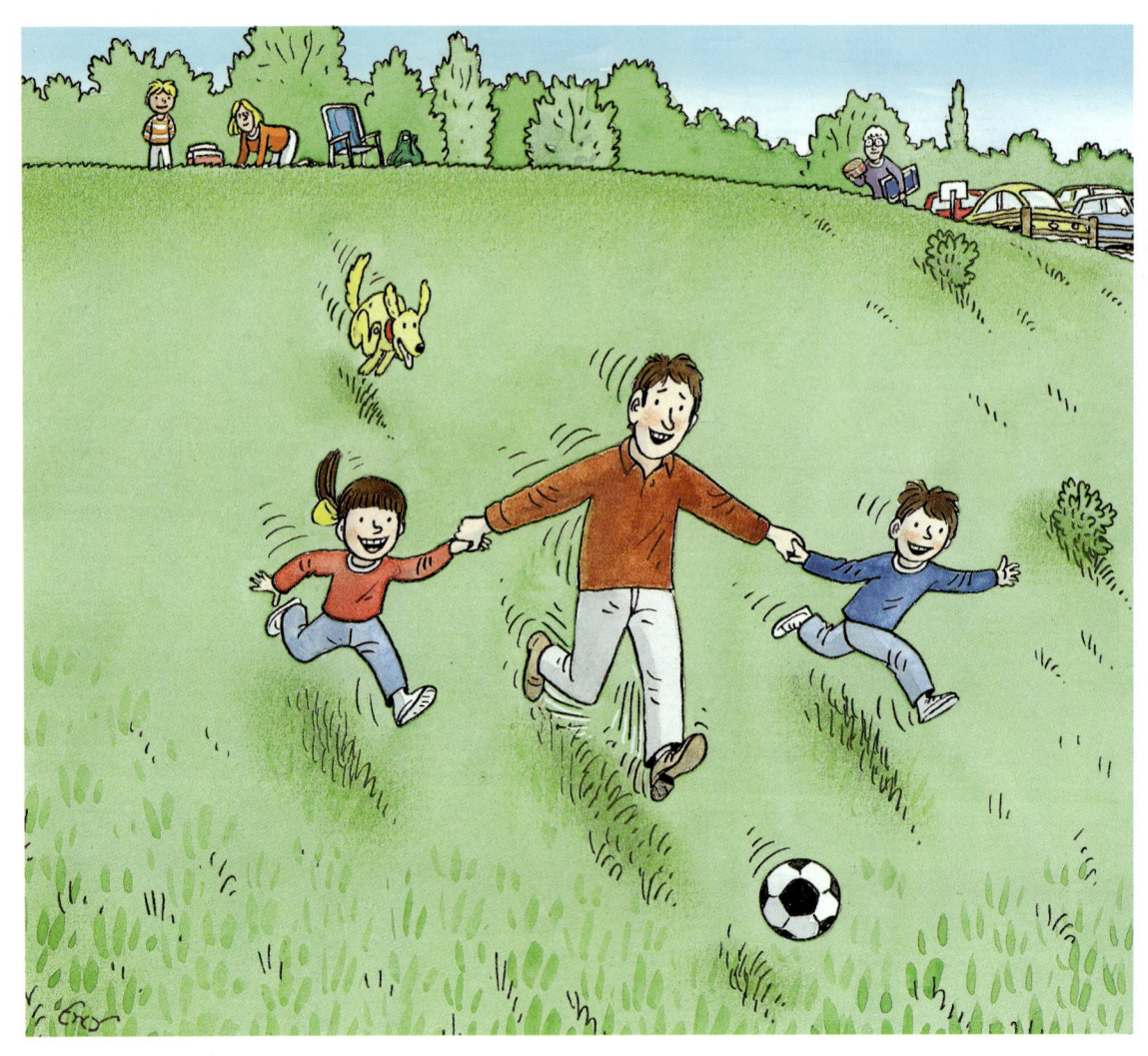

Biff, Chip and Dad ran
down the hill.

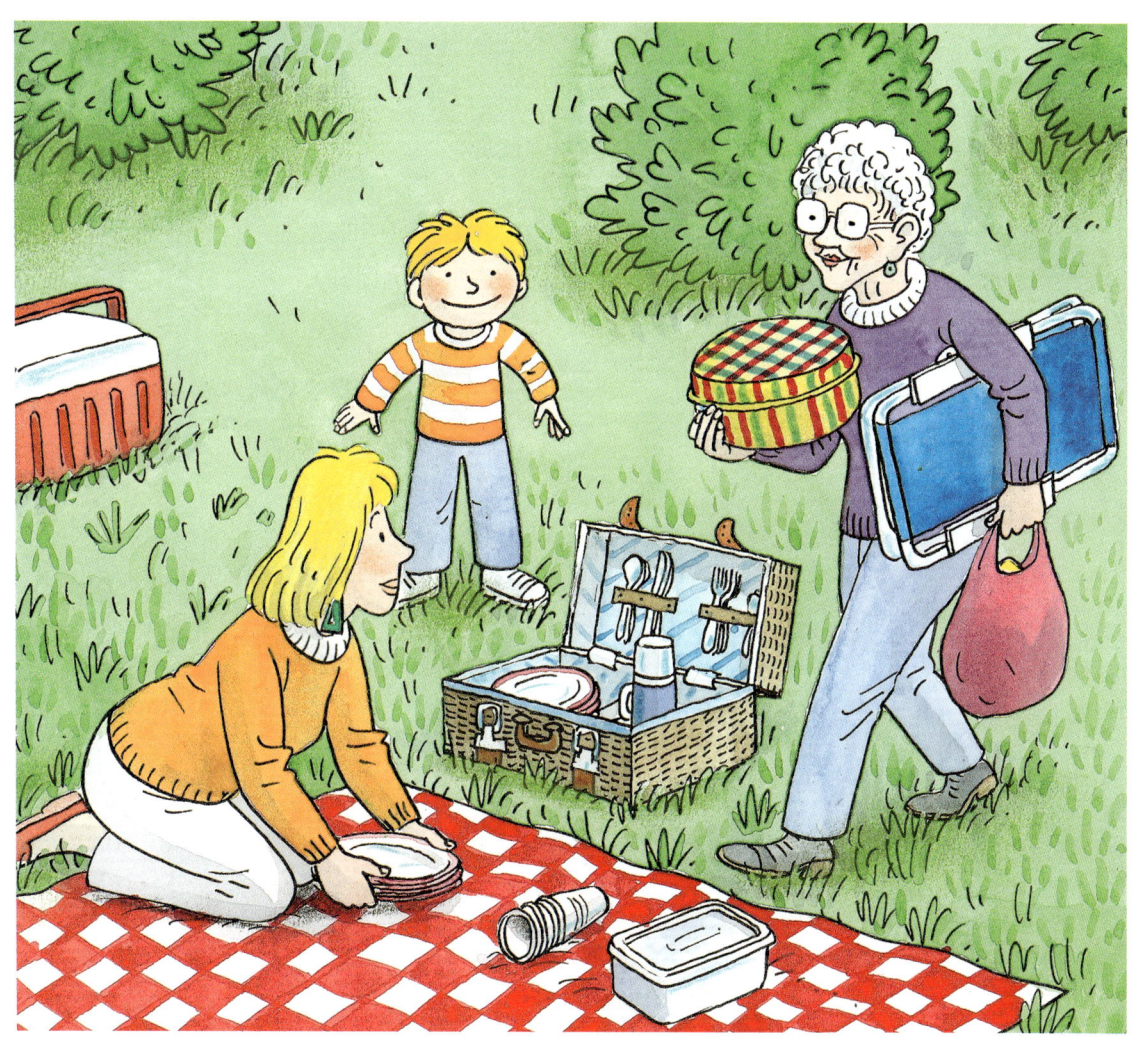

Gran had a big tin.

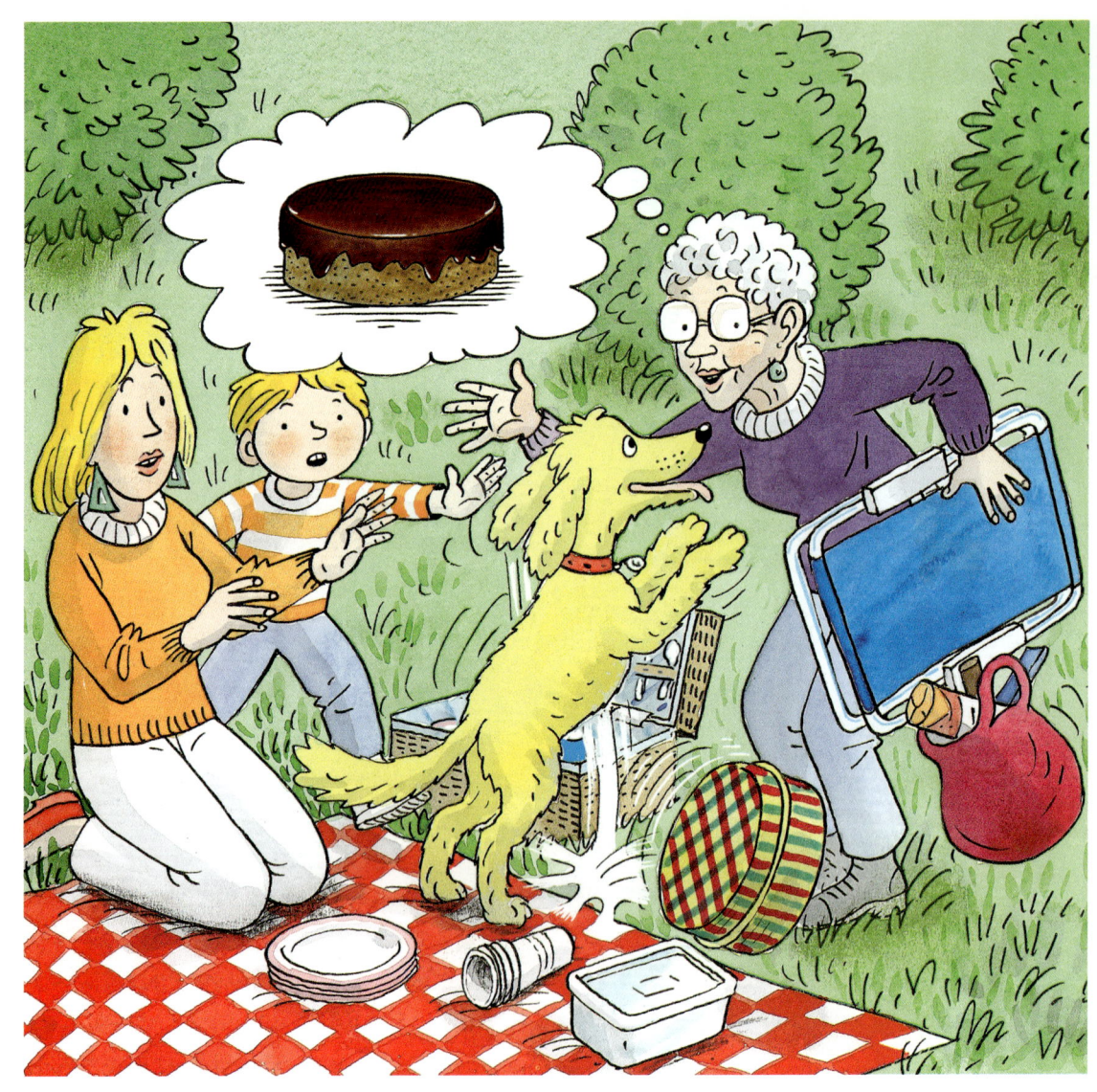

Floppy ran up to Gran.

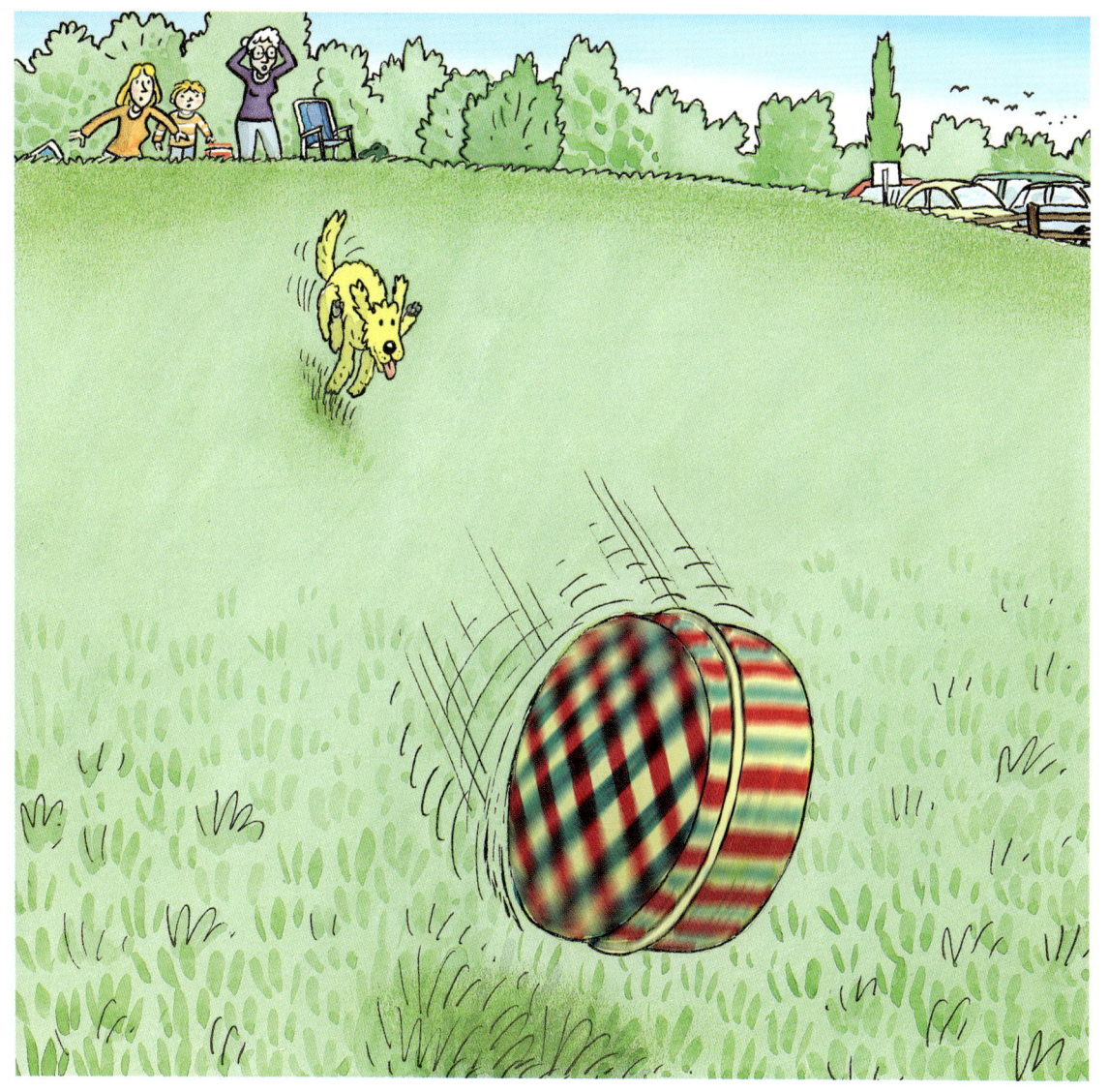

The tin went down the hill.

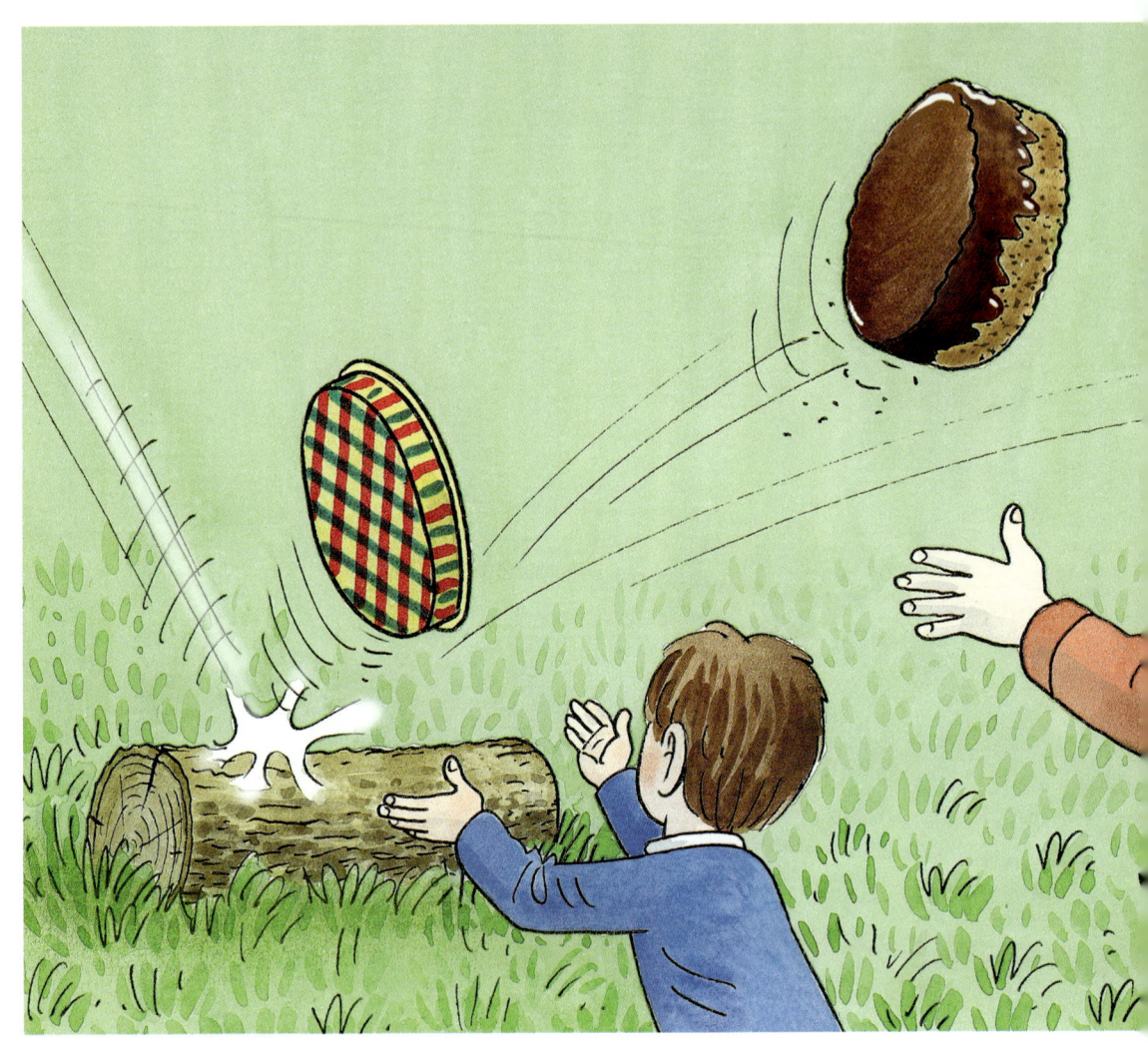

The tin hit a log.

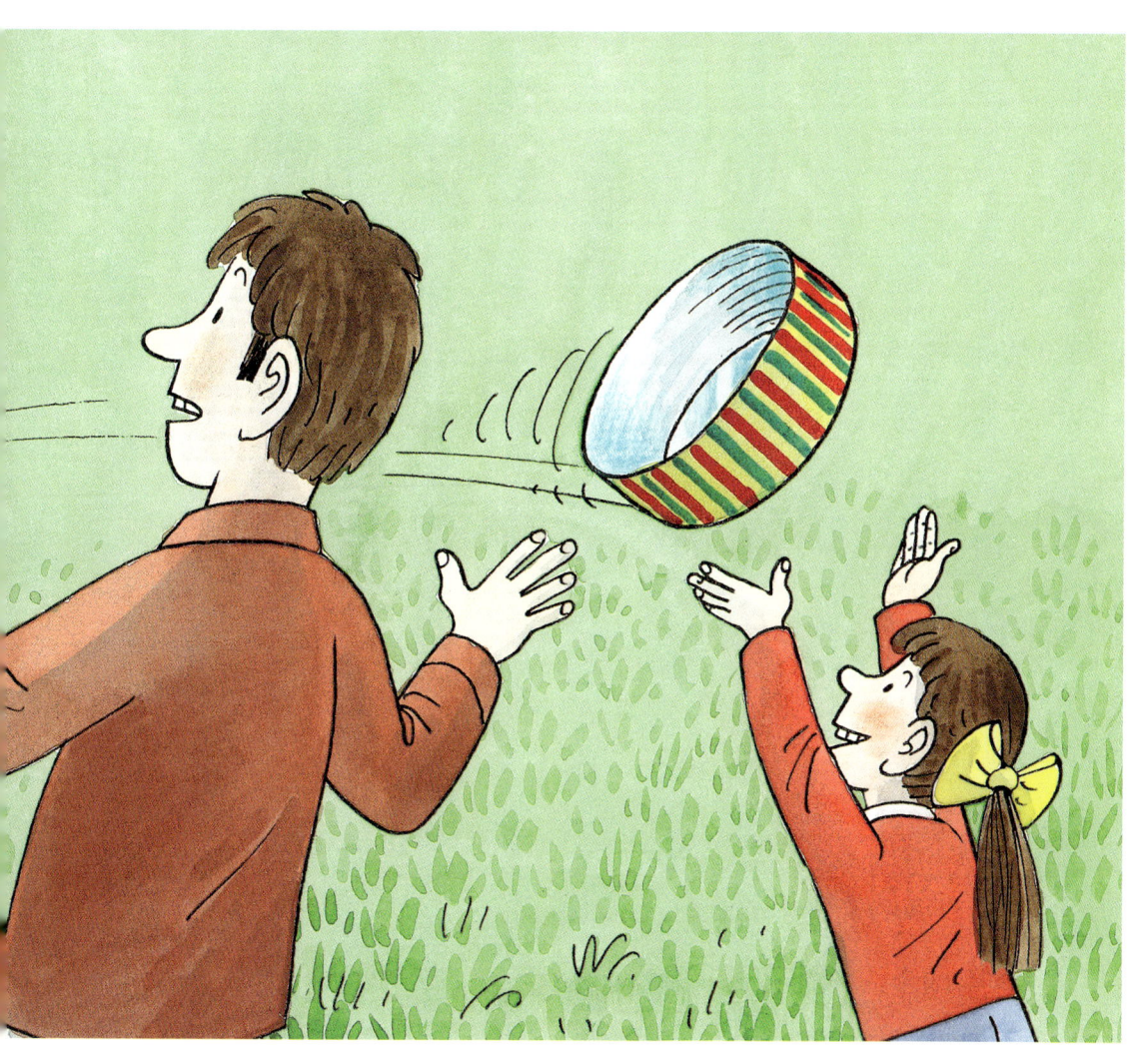

Chip got the lid. Biff got
the tin.

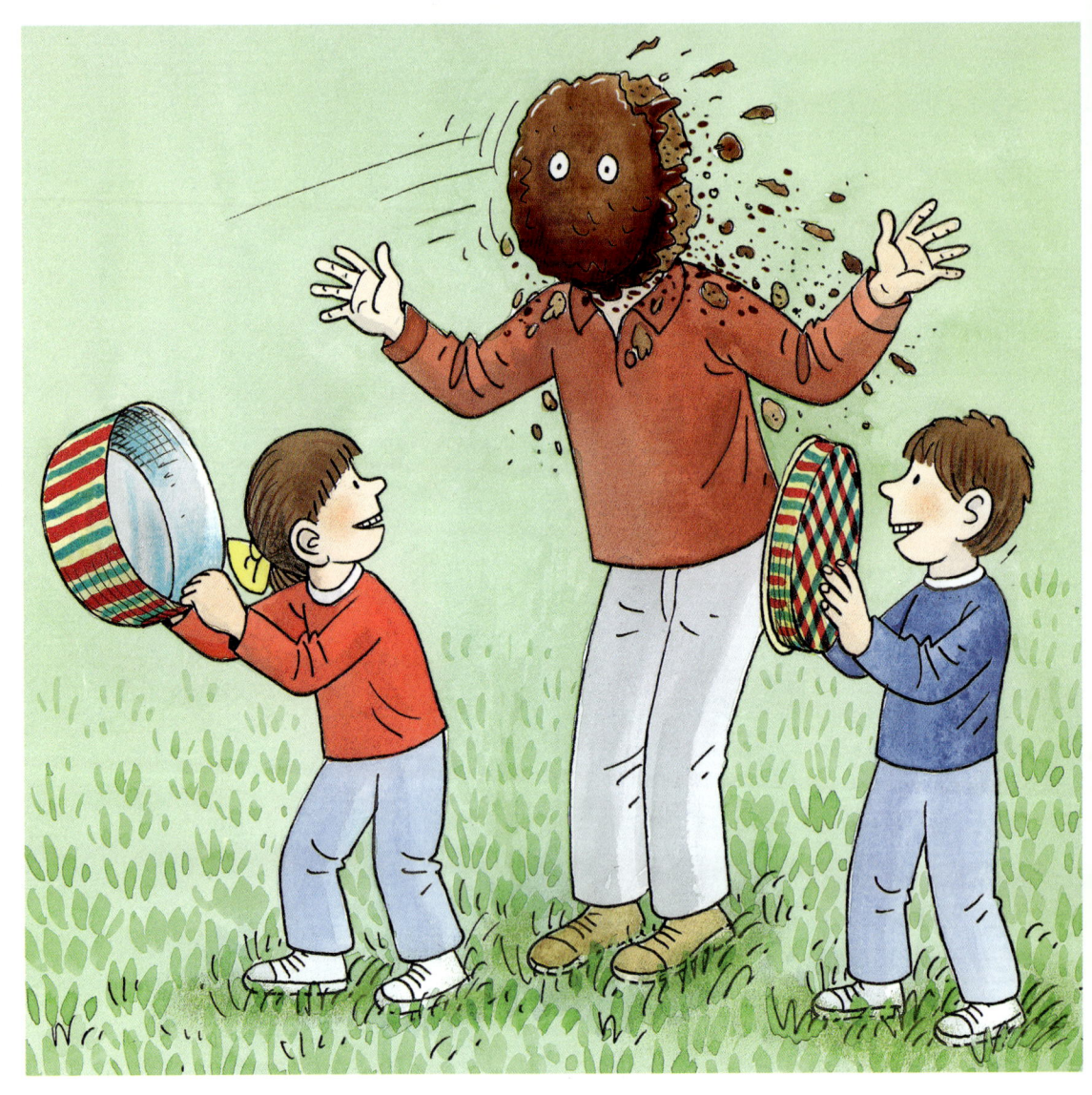

Oh no! Dad was in a mess.